I0559296

# Why Worship is Liturgical

A Brief Explanation of the Form and
Content of Traditional Christian Worship

**Jeffrey J. Meyers**

*Why Worship is Liturgical*
*A Brief Explanation of the Form and*
*Content of Traditional Christian Worship*
By Jeffrey J. Meyers

Copyright © 2024 Jeffrey J. Meyers
Athanasius Press
715 Cypress Street
West Monroe, Louisiana, 71291
www.athanasiuspress.org

Cover design and typesetting: Rachel Rosales

ISBN: 978-1-957726-15-1

Printed in the United States of America.

# Quick Reference

# Introduction

*Begin at the beginning, the King said, very gravely,*
*and go on till you come to the end: then stop.*
—Lewis Carroll, *Alice in Wonderland*

This little book is for those interested in learning more about Christian worship, specifically "traditional" Christian liturgical worship. By "traditional" I don't mean stodgy or boring or anachronistic and irrelevant. I know that is how the adjective is often used in some debates about worship, especially in modern America. And, of course, sometimes traditional services can indeed be conducted in a lifeless, slow, and dreary manner. How worship is "performed" is an important discussion to have, and I will say something about that later in the book.

   I should also note that by commending "traditional" worship I am not arguing for some sort of *histori-*

*cal reenactment event* on Sunday morning. Copying a sixth-century or a sixteenth-century liturgy and pasting it into a modern Sunday service is unwise for a host of reasons. That said, there will always be plenty of traditional words and actions in any Christian service that challenge those who have not grown up in church or are not familiar with the language of the Bible. Even so, stuffing a service with archaic, flowery language is not what makes worship traditional in the best sense of that word. For now, the reader should understand that by "traditional worship," I mean a Christian service that

1. follows a specific order or sequence,
2. climaxes with a Communion meal,
3. is saturated with Scripture (recited, prayed, sung, read aloud, and preached),
4. is led by Christian ministers,
5. requires coordinated congregational participation, and
6. glorifies the words of the minister and congregation with appropriate music and song.

Of course, I will explain these six points in more detail. But before I begin, I need to make another clarification. Not only is "traditional" not a bad word, but we should also not be afraid of the word "liturgy." No church can avoid liturgy. A church's liturgy is just all the rituals and rites the pastor and people engage in when they are assembled in God's presence as a church. The pastor and people speak, listen, sing, stand, sit, kneel, raise hands, bow heads, close eyes, open eyes, look, grasp, eat, drink, etc. in an ordered sequence. Hopefully, that ordered sequence communicates and embodies God's gracious gifts to us (Word and Sacrament), our grateful response to him, and our service to one another.

The big question is: why do we speak and sing with these particular words and in this specific sequence or order? Many churches today have adopted the informal style of American entertainment, with stages, bands, video screens, casually dressed ministers, and very little reflection on the order of the service. What is wrong with that "contemporary" form of worship? Why should we follow the more traditional practice of Christian worship? I hope to provide summary answers to those questions in this little book.

But here's one important answer to the "why" question up front: What we do when we gather for worship as the body of Christ cannot be relegated to some "religious" dimension of life, nicely segregated from the rest of human culture. Peter Leithart puts it this way as he begins his discussion of liturgy:

> Let's get something straight at the beginning: Liturgy isn't a marginal issue in Scripture. It is *the* issue. God created the world as liturgical space, and He intends to fill it with joyous, eternal worship. Liturgy is the Alpha and Omega of the biblical story. It's the reason God created human beings and everything else.[1]

## A Word to the Wise

Not every ritual action or liturgical practice that I describe in this book will be embodied in your local worship service. That's okay. Your church, for example, may not chant Psalms or pray responsive prayers as a congregation. Many churches are rediscovering the beauty and power of a more traditional worship service, but that rediscovery is ordinarily implemented over time and is presided over by a wise pastor that introduces changes prudently according to the needs of his own congregation. I have tried to make this book as generic as possible so that churches that practice liturgical worship will find this booklet a useful tool for helping their

---

1. *Theopolitan Liturgy* (Monroe, LA: Athanasius Press, 2019), 3.

people understand the biblical and practical benefits of the divine service.

If you are passionate about seeing some liturgical reformation in your own local church, then there are reasonable ways to go about starting a conversation with your pastor and leaders. What is not wise or effective is to start some sort of whisper campaign among your friends in the congregation about what you believe are the deficiencies in your local church's worship. And please don't mount a public campaign for changes in your church on social media. In other words, please don't use this little book to foment controversy in your church.

My intent is to provide a short, easy-to-read explanation for church members and visitors that practice a more liturgical Christian worship service. I want to help the inquiring visitor as well as the committed member know the biblical rationale for Christian corporate, Sunday worship. This should help everyone be able to worship intelligently, experiencing the fullness of reverent worship and praise. There are *reasons* why we do things the way we do—sound biblical, theological, and historical reasons. We are not simply following the dead, musty, liturgical traditions of some denomination. Neither are we clamoring to be "trendier than thou," like too many twenty-first century American churches seem to be doing these days. Drawing on the wisdom of the historic Church, especially the Reformation tradition, liturgical worship is firmly rooted and grounded in the Word of God.

For pastors, elders, and those training for the ministry I have included a very short bibliography to help you investigate these matters more thoroughly.

# Why Gather for Church on Sunday? Some Inadequate Answers

*The charge is feed my sheep not run experiments on my rats.*
—C.S. Lewis, *Letters to Malcolm*

There is a great deal of confusion today about the meaning and practice of Christian worship. Why does the church come together on Sunday? What is the purpose of a church service? What is supposed to happen? What part does the congregation have in the service? What is the role of the pastor?

One way to answer these questions would be to compose a list of the various activities that we typically engage in during the Sunday meeting. We assemble, sit, meditate, stand, hear, sing, pray, confess, praise, read, think, eat, drink, etc. Of course, with such a list we have not really answered the question: *why* do we do those things? To what end? For what purpose? What does all this hearing, speaking, standing, sitting, singing, praying, eating, and drinking accomplish? At the end of the service what will have happened? What will have changed, if anything? Are we there for an emotional experience? An educational lesson? What is the point of doing all this?

Moreover, if we can ask questions about the grand, overall meaning of the service, we can also ask about the form and content of each specific activity. Why do we do *these* things and not others? Why do we say these words and not others? Why do we *sing* some prayers and then *say* others? Why do we stand sometimes but sit for other parts of the service? Why do we sing certain hymns and songs, but leave others out of the service? Questions about the *sequence* of activities must also surface. Why do we do what we do in the *order* that we do them? Why does this come first and that second and this other thing third? Specific questions like these are intimately related to the question of the overall purpose of the whole assembly.

Perhaps I should make it more personal. Why do *you* come to church on Sunday morning? What are you hoping to do? What are you hoping to *give*? Or what do you anticipate *receiving*? What do you expect to be accomplished because of your being at church? Everyone comes for some reason. Do you come for the *appropriate* reasons?

Occasionally I walk into a room in my home or even get into my car and suddenly forget why I am there. Why did I come in here? Where am I going? My children call this "spacing out," as in "Dad's spacing out again, Mom." Of course, it normally only takes a few seconds to remember the reason I came into the room or got into my car. I can only imagine what would happen if the reason never came to me. What if I always walked into a particular room of my home without knowing why? Not knowing why one is in a specific place or doing a certain activity is not only embarrassing, but it is also abnormal.

Something like this happens to many Christians when they walk into their church service on Sunday morning. Unfortunately, unlike my temporary amnesia, there is often no recollection of the answer to the question "Why am I here?" Sometimes this is because the worshiper never had a clear understanding of the purpose of Sunday morning worship to start with. Some might have a ready answer to the question, but their reason for being in church might be tangential to the purpose of the service as a whole. They come to church because their parents taught them to come to church. They come to church because it is the thing to do on Sunday. Because their children need religious education. Because they meet friends at church. Because they can make productive business contacts. But if asked to explain the purpose of the Sunday service itself, they can do little more than repeat the opaque word "worship."

Before we look at the content of a Christian worship service, we must answer this crucial question: What is the *purpose* of our Lord's Day assembly? Why do we come to a church service on Sunday? Why are Christians called to assemble for a service? The answer to this key question will help explain why certain words and actions are included in the church's worship and will also determine the way in which the service is ordered from beginning to end. Unfortunately, there are serious disagreements among modern Christians about the purpose of Sunday worship. There are at least four different popular perspectives on the purpose of the Sunday worship service. In this chapter we will briefly analyze each proposed answer. This brief survey will prepare us for a fifth answer, one that we will begin to unpack in chapter two.

## Worship as Evangelism?

First, some feel that the purpose of the service ought to be evangelism, that outreach defines the chief purpose of the Sunday service. Accordingly, worship becomes a technique for evangelism. Too often, according to this view, *results* are what counts. The worship service is then evaluated based on the results obtained. At its worst, a church that adopts this posture may end up accepting whatever techniques that it judges to be *effective* in attracting unchurched people into the service. Churches that choose *evangelistic effectiveness* as the criteria by which they evaluate their services tend to look for ways to attract and entertain people, and they generally model their services after the broader cultural events (television talk shows, concerts, sitcoms, etc.).

It is important to stop and note that these pop "styles" are not neutral. They embody a distinctly American, twenty-first-century world view. Transforming the worship of the church using these cultural "styles" and the latest technological innovations in communication will affect the mindset and lifestyle of the community which submits to these popular forms. Form matters. Style = form. The way the Christian faith is embodied, communicated, lived, and sung is not neutral. Form is not something entirely indifferent. The *way* we pray and worship is inexorably related to *who* we are praying to and *what* we believe about the one we engage in prayer and praise. Style (form) and doctrine are mutually conditioning. Or at least they *ought* to be. What you believe will influence *how* you pray, worship, and sing. And conversely, the *way* in which you worship will shape *what* you believe. Tragically, some have not really thought through this issue. When we say things like, "I am not concerned with the worship style just the doctrine" or "worship style is merely a matter of taste, what's really important is the content of the sermon" or "as long as you believe correctly it doesn't really matter what style of worship you choose," it is frightening evidence of a very sloppy understanding of Christian worship.

These evangelism-driven church services are very carefully engineered to produce the desired results. Ed Dobson describes the seeker-church criteria for music selection:

> We wanted a musical style that would elicit a response. Unchurched people come to a service hesitantly. Their mind-set is 'you're not going to get me.' Their defenses are up. We felt that a style of music that would get them moving in a physical way (nodding heads and tapping feet) would help break down their defenses. This does not mean that the crowd are on their feet nodding

heads and clapping; they seldom clap during a song, but they always applaud at the end.[1]

There you have it: "breaking down their defenses" and the crowds always "applaud at the end." You see how marketing and emotional manipulation often play key roles in determining the shape of these services. The inside of the church may even look and feel like a concert hall (with a large band and choir up front), a movie theater (where everything is projected up onto a large screen), or an auditorium (with a "stage" up front). Typically, during the service the people are relatively passive: they function less like a congregation of active worshipers and more like an audience. Generally speaking, what happens in practice in these churches is that most of the traditional forms are jettisoned, and the church unashamedly embraces the dominant and omnipresent entertainment models so prominent in American culture.

### Worship as Education?

Another segment of the church believes that the Sunday service ought to be for the purpose of communi-

1. *Starting a Seeker Sensitive Service: How Traditional Churches Can Reach the Unchurched* (Grand Rapids: Zondervan, 1993), 42f.

cating truth. Education is the chief end of worship. Churches that have this emphasis tend to degenerate into lecture halls complete with overhead projectors and armies of note-taking members. Presbyterians and Bible churches often fall into this error. The sermon is elevated all out of proportion as the key element of worship. The communication of ideas and doctrines is the primary goal. Nothing else is of much importance in the service. Most of what comes before the sermon functions as "pre-game ceremonies" for the main event. People may like to sing, and singing may make them feel good, but they have not really thought through what purpose, if any, hymns and songs ought to have in the overall structure of the service—besides preparing the congregation emotionally for the sermon.

## Worship as Experience?

There are others who emphasize the experience of the congregation in worship. They believe that the Sunday service ought to produce some kind of beneficial emotional response in the people. If this is the purpose of the Sunday service, worship is reduced to sentimental and pious feelings. Pastors smile all the time and read poems from the pulpit to help the people feel good about themselves. For those who have embraced this philosophy of worship (a kind of liturgical *Pollyanna-*

*ism)*, the focus of the church is anthropological—that is, on *man*. I once phoned the office of a church whose biblical orthodoxy is questionable and heard the following answering machine message: "Remember God loves you *just the way you are*!" Of course, God loves his people despite what they are, through faith in Jesus Christ. But if engineering an experience is what is most important, then at all costs, people must leave the service feeling that they are O.K. and believing that everyone else is, too. Christianity is reduced to religious sentimentalism. In modern American church services, edification is cut loose from its doctrinal moorings and is blown about by every humanistic, trendy gust of psychological and sociological silliness.

**Worship as Praise?**
From this perspective the purpose of worship is to gather and give praise to God. Churches that emphasize praise as the goal of worship often style their services "celebrations." All those passages that call believers to "ascribe" or "give to the Lord the glory due to his Name" can be marshaled in support of the truth that the corporate service is a service of praise (Ps. 29:1-2; 96:7-8). This fourth conception of worship is much closer, but still not quite adequate to express the fullness of biblical worship. Certainly, there are numerous

passages that exhort us to "Praise the Lord" and to "worship" him. I would caution you, however, that in many cases the word "worship" has not served us very well. It is not the most helpful translation of words used to designate "bowing down" or "prostrating one-self" (e.g., Ps. 95:6). For example, when we are called to "prostrate" ourselves before God, this does not exactly correspond with the way we use the word "worship." To fall down before God is to allow oneself to be lifted up by him. It is to give oneself over to the Lord's ser-vice. In effect, falling down before God puts us in the position to be served by God. Much more, therefore, is often going on in these passages than merely ascribing "worth" or "praise" to God.

Often the giving of praise or glorifying of God is set over against the worshiper's expectation of *receiving* anything from God in church. Worship is what we *give* to the Lord, we are told. The super-spiritual-sounding assertion that "we just gather together to give praise to God, taking no interest in what we might get from him" is unbiblical, it may also easily slip into doxolog-ical hubris. Pastors and theologians are particularly vulnerable to this distortion of the purpose of worship. The slogan "we gather for worship *to give not to get*" has become something of an intellectual shibboleth in some circles. We love to beat other churches over the head with it. It makes us feel superior. As if we don't go to church because we *need* anything! We go to church to *give* God glory and honor. This kind of thinking is extremely dangerous.

For us, as dependent creatures of God, there can be no such thing as "disinterested praise." We simply cannot love or praise God for who he is apart from what he has given us or what we continue to receive from him. We are not his equals. The notion that pure love and worship of God can only be given when it is unmixed with all thoughts of what we receive, has no biblical grounding. To be sure, it sounds very spiritual and pious. It even comes across as self-denial. In fact, however, there is no such worship in the Bible for the simple fact that we cannot approach God as disinterested, self-sufficient beings. We are created beings. Dependent creatures. Beings who must continually *receive* both our life and redemption from God. Our "worship" of God, for this reason, necessarily involves our passive reception of his gifts as well as our thanksgiving and petitions. We cannot pretend that we do not depend upon him. We will always be receivers and petitioners before God. Our receptive posture is as ineradicable as our nature as dependent creatures. We must be served by him. Recognizing this reality is true spirituality. Opening oneself up to this reality is the first movement in our "worship"—indeed, the presupposition of all corporate worship. It is faith's posture before our all-sufficient, beneficent Lord. Praise alone can never be the exclusive purpose for our gathering together on the Lord's Day.

## Summary Evaluation

Obviously, there is some truth in each of these four perspectives. A Christian service that does not proclaim the Gospel to the lost (and saved!), engage the emotions of the congregation, teach God's word, and ascribe to God praise and honor will likely be a distorted, dangerously truncated service. All four of these opinions, however, err to the extent that they *reduce* the purpose of the church to one of these dimensions. Moreover, those who embrace one of the first four purposes tend to see the Sunday service as primarily a *technique* for producing a particular effect on the members of the congregation, either on their will, mind, or emotions.

All four of these dimensions—evangelism, preaching, edification, and praise—in and of themselves are very important. They each have their proper place in the worship service. But the overall purpose of a biblical worship service should not be *reduced* to any one of them. Moreover, the purpose (and practice) of our Lord's Day worship service must never degenerate into an attempt to engineer or manipulate some desired effect in the congregation. Worship must not be understood as a *technique*. "As C. S. Lewis said, 'The charge is feed my sheep not run experiments on my rats.' When worship is reduced to a pep rally for the pastor's latest crusade or to a series of events that contain the minister's own hidden agenda, our concern for worship is called into question."[2] Every conception and form of liturgy that focuses on man will eventually degenerate into intellectual or psychological manipulation.

2. William H. Willimon, *Worship as Pastoral Care* (Nashville: Abingdon Press, 1979), 17.

# The Biblical Purpose
# of the Divine Service

*When you come together as a church...*
—1 Corinthians 11:18

What, then, is the purpose of our service on the Lord's Day? According to the Scriptures, in corporate Christian worship, members of the believing congregation are engaged by the Spirit and drawn into the Father's presence as living sacrifices in Christ. "Through Christ we . . . have access in one Spirit to the Father" (Eph. 2:18). Our reasonable liturgy, the apostle Paul says, is to "offer ourselves as living sacrifices" (Rom. 12:1-2). On the Lord's Day God himself visits his people in judgment and salvation, reconstituting and restoring them for life in his presence and work in his kingdom. In response to God's initiative—his drawing near to us—we confess, thank, praise, pray, and eat together as renewed creatures who through the Spirit are enabled to give unto our Lord the glory due his Name.

## God Serves Us First

In view of the one-sided emphasis in some Christian circles—that the congregation gathers to *give* praise to God and not to *get* anything—we must expose the lopsided, impoverished nature of this teaching. We have been told by well-meaning teachers, even some theologians, that it is downright wrong to come to church in order to *get* something. A popular slogan has it, for example, that Presbyterian/Reformed worship stands apart from other theologies of worship in that we don't come to *get* anything but to *give* praise and honor and glory to God. This conception must not be permitted to go unchallenged.

First, and above all, we are called together in order to get, to receive. This is crucial. The Lord gives, we receive. Since faith is receptive and passive in nature, "faith-full" worship must be about receiving from God. He gives, and by faith we receive. We are given his forgiveness, his Word, his nourishment, his benediction, etc. We come as those who receive *first* and then, second, only in reciprocal exchange do we give back what is appropriate as grateful praise and adoration.

More and more, I am discovering how crucial (at least in our current situation) such a conception of worship is. Too often Christian liturgy is described first of all as the "work of the people." While I do not deny that we "work" during worship, I do regard this definition as dangerously one-sided. Whatever we "do" in worship must always be the faithful *response* to God's gifts of forgiveness, life, knowledge, and glory—gifts we graciously receive from the Lord in the service! Much of what goes by the name "contemporary" worship has evacuated the Sunday service of God's service to man. It is all about what *we* do. The reduction of Christian worship to "praise" and "giving worth to God" by well-intentioned pastors desirous of purging the church of superficial worship forms will only continue to feed the very thing that they oppose.

For example—to name one side-effect of this kind of thinking—the disappearance of the pastor as the Lord's representative and spokesman, the ordained man through whom the Lord gives, is tied to this kind of mentality. Many pastors no longer lead the worship service. One friend described the typical way pastors now "lead" a Sunday morning service as "MC-ing" the event. He's a jovial, laid-back, joke-telling, casual-dressed guy that keeps people engaged with what is going on up front on the stage. This departure of the leadership of the pastor in contemporary worship follows from the kind of one-sided conception of the Lord's Day service that I have been critiquing. If what the people are doing in worship is merely getting together to praise and pray and offer God all kinds of human devotion, then we can all just do it together and anyone can lead us. If, however, *the Lord himself* is meeting us and giving us his gifts, then the ordained minister will be prominent so that the people can be left in no doubt that it is the Lord himself who is speaking, forgiving, baptizing, offering us food and drink, and finally blessing us and sending us out into the world to further his kingdom.

That is not to say that the Lord serves us in worship *exclusively* through the pastor, since the Lord is at work even in the corporate praying, reciting, and the singing of the congregation. How many times have we been truly served by God as we listened to and joined in with the united voices of the church in prayer and praise? The Lord, then, serves us on the Lord's Day as his Spirit speaks through both the voice of the minister as well as the voices of his people. We should never lose sight of the primacy of the Lord's service *to us* when we gather before him on the Lord's Day.

## The Lord's Service

Moreover, the terminology we use to describe what happens on the Lord's Day can be confusing. We've inherited the designation "worship service," which, to my mind, tends to introduce confusion. "Service" comes from the Latin *servitium*, as in *servitium Dei* ("the service of God" or "God's service"). This older way of designating the Christian liturgy is delightfully ambiguous. In the "Divine Service" or "the service of God" who's serving whom? Is God serving us? Or are we serving God? Or is it both? Classically, the "Divine Service" was thought to include both God's service to us and our service to God. Even so, our fathers in the faith considered God's service to us (the forgiveness of sins, the ministry [service!] of the Word, the Sacraments, etc.) as primary and our service to him as a secondary response.

But this emphasis may be lost when we designate our corporate, Sunday assembly "worship." This term comes to us by way of the Anglo-Saxon word "worthship," which simply meant to accord someone his proper worth. What we appear to be emphasizing with this term is not God's gifts and ministry to us through his Word and Sacraments, but our ascribing "worth" to him. We are too ready to accept the misleading definition of liturgy as "the work of the people," which is in fact only half of the story, and the second half at that! What happens on Sunday is the continuation of the service of the ascended Lord Jesus for his people. "For who is greater: the one at the table or the one who serves? The one at the table, surely. Yet here am I among you as the one who serves!" (Luke 22:27; see also Matt. 20:28; John 13:5-16; Phil. 2:7-8).

Allow me to hammer this point home. Without this understanding, our worship inevitably degenerates into paganism with a Christian veneer. We must recognize our service is *not* first of all *for* God. We first receive *from* God, then, *secondly*, we give back *to* him with gratitude precisely that which he graciously continues to give us. He stands in no need of our service or praise. He has not created us primarily so as to get glory for himself, but to distribute and share the fullness of his glory with his creatures. He is not like the pagan gods who need selfishly to suck up as much of the glory and praise as they can. With the true God, the determination of the amount of glory possessed by him and us is not a zero-sum game. If he has all glory, that does not imply we have none. If we possess glory, it does not come at the expense of his glory. When we refuse to acknowledge the source of our glory and assert our own *over against* his, we fall under the condemnation of the prophets. Thomas Howard rightly challenges this distortion:

> If God alone is all-glorious, then no one else is glorious at all. No exaltation may be admitted for any other creature, since this would endanger the exclusive prerogative of God. But this is to imagine a paltry court. What king surrounds himself with warped, dwarfish, worthless creatures? The more glorious the king, the more glorious are the titles and honors he bestows. The plumes, cockades, coronets, diadems, mantles, and rosettes that deck his retinue testify to one thing alone, his own majesty and munificence. He is a very great king to have figures of such immense dignity in his train, or even better, to have raised them to such dignity. These great lords and ladies, mantled and crowned with the highest possible honor and rank are, precisely, his vassals. This glittering array is his court! All glory to him, and in him, glory and honor to these others.[1]

It is this cruder form of the doctrine that is too often the popular view. If anyone has an ounce of glory,

---

1. *Evangelical Is Not Enough* (Nashville: Thomas Nelson, 1984), 87.

then God must confiscate it. This is pagan, not Christian. Rather, we must say that if anyone has an ounce or two pounds of glory, it has been bestowed by God from the plentitude of his own glory and so all glory in the world must ultimately redound to him. "For of him and through him and to him [are] all things, to whom [be] glory forever. Amen" (Rom. 11:36).

### Gift and Response

Christian worship provides the occasion for God's service to the church, that is, in the liturgy *God serves us* by granting us the gifts of the kingdom, which includes, but is not limited to knowledge. We gather to receive. The Lord gives. So, for example, I believe the diminishing place of the pastor in the Sunday service corresponds to the deformation of the service from what God does for us to what we do before God. When the robed pastor is prominent the people are left in no doubt that God is speaking and acting through the instrumentality of the office of the Ministry to deliver his gifts to the congregation.

God's operations on us come first and our actions are in grateful response to God's gracious activity. Note: I do not mean to suggest that our response is not also included in God's gracious provision in Christ. It is. It is not as if God works but then stops just where our human response begins. Rather, God's grace includes precisely that human response to the extent that our human response takes place "in Christ." God is at work in us even when we are at work praising him. We "work" at thanking and praising him because he is at work in us (1 Cor. 12:3; Rom. 8:26; Phil. 2:13). The entire process of Christian worship can only be performed as we are graciously given to participate in the priestly work of Jesus Christ by the power of the Spirit. Our offering of ourselves as Christians will always be a participation in Jesus' own priestly offering of his humanity to the Father in the Spirit.

If the Church's worship is the place where God himself distributes his life-giving Word and Sacraments, if it is the occasion for God to *serve* the congregation, then with this understanding we can, to some degree, transcend the rigid dichotomy regarding the purpose of the Sunday service—is it for evangelism or worship? Why do we have to choose between one or the other? Is worship for the people of God or unbelievers? Well, primarily for the people of God, but if unbelievers are present, they may be served as well. If through the liturgy God graciously delivers gifts of forgiveness, life, and salvation, then he offers them to everyone present—the people of God as well as those who are not yet part of his people. Inasmuch as the

Lord's Day service is the place and time where God comes through his Word and Sacrament to serve people, it is obviously beneficial to both. The Spirit can enliven any unbeliever present and use his Word as it is read, prayed, sung, and preached to bring them new life. What else is this but evangelism?

Therefore, the fundamental purpose of the corporate Sunday service is to *receive* by faith God's gracious service in Christ and then to *respond* with thanksgiving in union with Christ *worshiping* the Living God. This is what we call "covenant renewal worship."

# Covenant Renewal Worship

*Do this as my memorial.* —1 Corinthians 11:25

Why do we use the word "covenant" to describe the renewal that God accomplishes in the service? The Bible uses the word "covenant" over three hundred times in the Old and New Testaments to describe the precise nature of God's relationship to his people. God enters into, remembers, and renews his covenant with his people (Gen. 6:18; Deut. 5:3; Ezek. 16:60; Heb. 8:10; Luke 1:72; 22:20, etc.). The people must not break but remember and renew their covenant with God (1 Chron. 16:15; Psalm 103:18; Hos. 6:7, etc.). In our American cultural climate we need to stress that our "relationship" with God is not merely a "personal relationship" but a *covenantal* relationship. This is an important qualification. The phrase "personal relationship" is used rather freely in popular culture. It usually describes very informal, often casual relationships between people. Popular television sitcoms often celebrate "personal relationships." These kinds of relationships can be *on* one day and *off* the next. They involve no formal or binding responsibilities. They bend, sway, and stretch according to the desires of the individuals involved in these "relationships." They have no objective shape or form. This is not the case with covenantal relationships in the Bible.

God's personal relationship with us takes the *form* of a covenant. The "covenant" *structures* God's personal relationship with us. We do not merely have a personal relationship with Jesus. That might mean almost anything. To some it simply means that Jesus is going to take them to heaven when they die because they prayed a prayer or walked an aisle in church. To others it might mean more, so that they talk to him when they are in trouble or come to church to think about him occasionally. A covenantal relationship, however, is a formal, binding relationship between God and us. Like marriage (which is a human covenant modeled after God's covenant with us, Eph. 5:22ff.), God's covenant with us has a definitive shape and content. The covenant contains promises that are made to be kept (by God and us), privileges that we are to enjoy, and stipulations that we must strive to obey. Furthermore, there is a distinctive way of renewing covenantal relationships in the Bible, and that is by way of *sacrifice* (Gen. 8:20-9:17; Gen. 15:8-18a; Exod. 24:4-11; 34:15; Lev. 2:13; 24:1-8; Num. 18:19; 1 Kings 3:15; Ps. 50:5; Luke 22:20; Heb. 9:15, 18; 9:20; 12:24; 13:20).

This means that we could also call our corporate service "sacrificial worship" because God renews his covenant with us by way of sacrifice. That is, the Lord himself graciously gathers us together as the church to draw us anew into his glorious, life-giving presence by way of sacrifice. What is this "way of sacrifice"?

### Worship as Sacrifice

The word "liturgy" is a Bible word and ought not to scare us, if we properly understand and qualify its meaning. In Romans 12:1, for example, we are urged, in response to God's mercy, to offer our bodies as living sacrifices. Such a course, we are told, is holy and pleasing to God; it is our "reasonable service." The word translated "service" (or "worship" in some translations) is the Greek word *latreia*, which refers to the sacrificial "service" or "liturgy" by which the worshiper presents himself to God (Phil. 3:3; Heb. 9:9; 10:2; 12:28).

In Acts 13:2, for example, the Antioch church's worship on the Lord's Day is described as follows: "On one occasion, while they were engaged in the liturgy of the Lord and were fasting, the Holy Spirit spoke to them" (my translation). Many newer translations speak of the church "ministering" to the Lord. The word "ministering" means "serving," and the Greek word is *leitourgeo* which refers to public, congregational service—whether God's service to the people or the people's before God is hard to know. The language of Acts 13:2 ("the Lord's liturgy" or "service") is ambiguous, maybe purposefully so in order that both God's service to the assembly and the people's service to God is included. Nevertheless, the assembled congregation at Antioch was engaged in what we would today call a "worship service." We gather on the Lord's Day as the church, not to serve ourselves, but to be served by God and to serve him.

In Hebrews 9:6 the word "liturgy" (*latreia*) refers to the ceremonies or rites of the Aaronic priests in Israel's Tabernacle and Temple. After Jesus' death and resurrection and the outpouring of the Holy Spirit on the day of Pentecost, God's people as a whole are priests. United to Jesus, our high priest, the entire congregation has sanctuary access as "saints." Therefore, as New Covenant priests, the people of God perform priestly service (*latreia*). This mode of "sacrificial living" should characterize our daily lives, to be sure, but on the Lord's Day there is a special sense in which we are gathered together by God as the body of Christ in order to be drawn into God's presence as "living sacrifices." If we are not used to thinking this way, Robert S. Rayburn's explanation may help:

> Part of the reason why so many Christian worship services have no logic, no order, no movement, is because those who superintend those services of worship have not paid attention to the Bible's main instruction in the formation of a worship service *because that instruction is found in the Old Testament*. . . . It is this disregard for the importance of what is done in the worship of God and the order or logic with which it is done that has led to the common pejorative use of the words 'liturgy' and 'liturgical' in many evangelical and even Reformed circles. This is a mistake in more ways than one. Every church service is a liturgy, if it has various elements in some arrangement. That is what liturgy is. Liturgical churches are churches that have *thought* about those elements and their proper order. Non-liturgical churches are those which have not. It is no compliment to say that a church is a non-liturgical church. It is the same thing as saying it is

a church that gives little thought to how it worships God.[1]

The meaning of "liturgy," therefore, according to the New Testament, is intimately connected with the biblical practice of "offering" and "sacrifice." More important than finding the word "liturgy" in the Bible, is the recognition that God has established the *way* of approaching him. God's way of graciously drawing us into his presence is not arbitrary, but follows a predictable *sequence* that is controlled by his holy and merciful character as the Triune God. According to the New Testament, the way or order in which God draws the sacrificial animals into his presence in the Old Testament symbolizes God's appointed way of drawing sinful human beings into his holy but life-giving presence. This is the way of sacrifice. Sacrifice answers the question: "How are we drawn into God's presence?"

1. Robert S. Rayburn, "Worship From the Whole Bible," in *The Second Annual Conference on Worship: The Theology and Music of Reformed Worship, February 23-25, 1996* (Nashville, TN: Covenant Presbyterian Church, 1996), 22-23.

**Drawing Near to God**

In the Hebrew Scriptures the "sacrifice" or "offering" is called *qorban*, which means "that which is brought near" (Lev. 1:2; 2:1; 3:1-2; 4:23; 5:11; 7:38). Biblical sacrifice is not a technique invented by man to secure something from God. Rather, God has graciously provided man with a way of entering into his presence, and that way is the way outlined in the sacrificial system of Israel. The worshiper is mercifully *brought near* to God's presence by means of the substitute/representative animal (*qorban*). Ultimately this is the way of Jesus Christ's life, death, resurrection, and the resulting incorporation of his (and our) humanity into the Trinitarian family life of the Godhead. Jesus Christ offered himself by the Spirit to the Father once for us all, *and* we, too, united to Christ, must follow his lead. By the Spirit we are drawn into God the Father's presence through the priestly work of Jesus Christ. This is what happens every Lord's Day in the worship service. This is the way of sacrificial worship—united to Christ we are not only brought together by the Spirit, but by the same Spirit we are drawn into the Father's presence by cleansing, consecration, and communion.

This has enormous implications for issues surrounding the *order* of the service. Even though this dimension of biblical worship has been almost totally neglected in some Protestant traditions (the emphasis instead being on the "elements" of worship), I believe that discovering the biblical order or sequence of man's approach to God in the service may be the key to resurrecting a powerful Bible-based liturgy in our churches. Most pastors and theologians do have a proper sense of how a worship service should be ordered, but they may not have thought through why this order is appropriate. I believe that the traditional Christian liturgical order arose in the early church from a gut-level familiarity with the biblical way of approaching God, even if church theologians have not always explicitly identified the biblical source of their intuitions. What I offer is a reasonable biblical explanation of the order of Christian worship as the corporate, sacrificial, covenant renewal service of God.

**The Three Crucial Steps in the Service**
Without going into too much detail, the basic order of sacrificial/covenantal worship ought to be clear in your mind before we proceed to explain the service in detail. You might think about the three major "sections" or "movements" within the service as three "steps." The movement of the service is something of an "ascent" into God's presence along the pathway he has established. (In some sense it is also God's "descent"

as well, but we will discuss that aspect when we come to the Communion meal.) Just as every sacrificial animal passed through three "zones" and underwent three major "operations" on its way up the altar and into the presence of God, so also the human worshiper travels the same sacrificial pathway up the "holy mountain" into God's presence.

An "altar" in the Bible is a communion site, the place where God meets with and communes with man. Altars in the Israelite sacrificial system were symbolic holy mountains (like Mt. Sinai) where the worshipper, symbolized by the animal, ascended into God's presence (the fiery presence on top of the altar). By faith we understand our progress during the Lord's Day service to be God's gracious drawing of us into his presence, making us fit, in Christ, for fellowship with him.

The three steps are cleansing, consecration, and communion. These are just convenient alliterative labels that we attach to the three major operations performed on the sacrificial animals as the Lord drew them (and the worshipers symbolized by them!) into his presence. Each sacrificial animal is always 1) slaughtered and its blood splashed on the altar (cleansing), then 2) washed, skinned, cut up, and arranged on the altar grill (consecration), and finally 3) turned into smoke and incorporated into God's fiery presence on top of the altar as food (communion). This is the sacrificial pathway/liturgy that every animal/worshiper experienced as God drew him near.

Contrary to popular Christian opinion, the New Testament does not abrogate sacrifice, but rather, Jesus Christ fulfills and establishes the genuine meaning and practice of sacrifice and offering. Sacrificial images and rites are part of the *central core* of the biblical revelation concerning the personal relations between God and man (from Gen. 3:21 through Rev. 21:22-27). The sacrificial language and imagery is not merely fulfilled in the work of Jesus Christ, but also serves to define and shape the life of the believer in Christ. In the Hebrew Scriptures both the work of Christ *and* the work of the believer in Christ is prophetically couched in the symbolic structures of animal sacrificial rites and all that accompanies them—altars, bowls, knifes and other assorted hardware. In the New Testament the Old Testament sacrificial typology is fulfilled *by* Christ and *in* the believer, who is united to Christ by faith. In union with Christ—who offered himself as *the* Sacrifice (capital "S")—we not only have the penalty for sin removed, but we are also *being made into acceptable sacrifices ourselves* by faith. The promise is that if we by faith offer ourselves to the Father through Christ in the

Spirit we will become what we are meant to become as men and women re-made in the image of God.

In addition to the three "steps" taken by (or "operations" performed on) each sacrificial animal, there were also three types of sacrifices that were part of the normal tabernacle/temple liturgy of Old Testament worship: a purification sacrifice, an ascension (or whole burnt) sacrifice, and a fellowship sacrifice (the "sacrifice of peace"). The inauguration of the priesthood of Aaron in Leviticus 9 shows us the order in which each of these sacrifices were offered in the tabernacle liturgy. Each specific type of sacrifice highlights one of the three major operations:

1.  The Purification highlights and expands on the cleansing or purification dimension of sacrificial offerings. That's why it is called the *purification* offering. The act of the slaughter and the display of the blood is accented. For example, Lev. 16 (the day of atonement) is an elaborate purification offering where the act of confession and forgiveness is highlighted. The other two aspects are there, but downplayed.

2.  The Ascension expands on the element of *consecration* and *ascension* of the animal/worship-

er into God's presence. That is why it is named *'olah* (Hebrew for "ascension"). The animal is caused to ascend. The ascension sacrifice highlights the acts of skinning, cutting up, washing, and then the transformation of the entire representative animal by fire and its incorporation into the cloud of God's special presence on the altar.

3. The Communion or the Sacrifice of Peace expands on the element of union and *communion* with God, which is present in all the sacrifices, but is highlighted in this offering. The *food* aspect of sacrifice is emphasized. In the communion offering, fellowship and peace with God are not merely symbolized by the sacrifice being turned into smoke and assimilated into the glory cloud, but here fellowship with God is communicated by means of a common meal. There is purification and consecration in the liturgy of this sacrifice, but the focus in this offering is on the communal meal that the worshiper enjoys with Yahweh, the priests, and his family by means of the sacrifice. The worshiper experiences the gift of peace from the Lord at a table with other worshippers.

Furthermore, these three types of sacrifices are always offered in the same order: purification (cleansing), ascension (consecration), and peace (communion meal). Thus, we have *revealed* an order or liturgy of approach to God not only in each individual sacrifice, but the same path is manifest in the liturgical order by which the three ordinary sacrifices were regularly offered.

Another biblical way to think about these three steps in the service is to consider God's three ways of serving us or God's three gifts given to us on the Lord's Day. These are his gifts of glory, wisdom, and life. They correspond to the three hidden gifts in the Ark of the Covenant locked away in the Tabernacle's Most Holy Place: Aaron's rod with almond blossoms (glory), a copy of the Torah (wisdom), and a pot of manna (life). What was hidden in the Old Testament is now revealed in Christ (Exod. 16:31-34; Eph. 3:9; Col. 1:26; 2:3; Heb. 9:3-4; Rev. 2:17). He is the final and faithful high priest (the greater Aaron). He is the Word of God incarnate (the true wisdom of God). And Jesus is the heavenly manna, the bread of life come down from heaven to give life to the world (John 6:35). These three gifts correspond with the three ways in which God serves us as he draws us along the sacrificial pathway into his presence.

## The Order of a Christian Liturgy

During the first stage of the service God reconstitutes us in our personal, covenantal relationship with him. We are granted the gift of the forgiveness of sins and the clothing of the righteousness of Christ. We receive from God a renewal of our standing in his presence. We are fully restored as priests in Christ who have the authority to come boldly into the Father's presence by the Spirit. This corresponds to the first operation performed on the sacrificial animal—he is executed and his blood must soak the altar from top to bottom, thus opening the door in heaven from God to man. It also correlates with the "sin (or purification) offering," which is the *first* sacrifice when all three of the normal sacrifices are offered. Blood must be shed. The animal (worshiper) must die. The blood must then be applied on the altar (the way of ascent into God's presence) from top to bottom. The presence of the blood opens up a pathway into God's holy presence. No one dares come into God's presence without confessing their sins and re-appropriating the efficacy of the shed blood of Christ. There is no sanctuary access without confession and forgiveness.

Secondly, God speaks to us from his Word as the pastor explains and applies the Bible. Listening to the Word of God, we hear the Spirit's guidance for our lives. The double-edged sword of the Word chops us up and rearranges us as living sacrifices (Lev. 1:6). The sword of the priest, which earlier had executed the animal, now serves to prepare him for his transformation into fire on the altar. The sword and the fire on the altar do not destroy, but transform. The judgment has been rendered by the knife when the animal was killed. The fact that more happens to the animal than merely his death tells us that from that point on the animal is being made fit for God's presence. The final operation is performed when the animal is transformed into smoke on top of the altar and is transported into God's glory-cloud presence. The New Testament makes clear that the transforming sword of God is the Word which the fiery Spirit uses to transfigure Christ's people (Heb. 4:12). The sermon occupies the major place in this second step of sacrificial worship. We should note that the tribute or meal (grain) offering, which symbolizes the offering of the worshiper's work, is placed on top of the animal sacrifice just as it is being turned into smoke. This corresponds to the collection of tithes and offerings from the people after the sermon.

The third and climactic step in the sacrificial/ covenantal renewal liturgy is the Lord's Supper. In the Old Covenant this was symbolized when the animal is turned into smoke, ascends, and is assimilated into

God's glory cloud, which corresponds to the worshiper's being drawn into the nearest possible relation to God. This union with God may also be seen in the third and last sacrifice offered in the liturgical sacrificial sequence—the sacrifice of peace/fellowship. There can be no more intimate symbol of the close fellowship of God and man than the covenant meal. From Genesis to Revelation the meal remains the preeminent symbol of God's intimate love and presence with mankind in Christ. Having been reconciled, God and man are at peace around the Table. What we call the "altar" in our Bibles would be better translated as "communion site." It's the place were God and man, as well as the community, come together.

In our order of worship once the congregation has received the forgiveness of sins and experienced the transforming ministry of the Word of God, then the Lord provides them with the assurance of peace—a covenantal memorial meal. Sacrifices are "food" (Lit. "bread" in Hebrew) for God (Lev. 3:11, 16; 21:6; Num 28:2; and in Lev. 6:10 the fire is said to "eat" the sacrifice), which means that the Lord delights in those whom he draws near. God does not *need* food (Ps. 50:7-15), but he takes pleasure in "tasting" his people. Being eaten is symbolic of being incorporated into fellowship with God.

Based on this analysis, we can now offer a synopsis of the service. The congregation will be served by God as they move from prostration (confessional obeisance in response to being called into God's presence) to standing (praise for God's renewed forgiveness) to sitting (in order to hear the Word) to reclining at the Table (to enjoy table fellowship with God). The basic three-fold pattern of God's service to us may be outlined as follows:

God Cleanses Us
God Consecrates Us by Teaching Us
God Communes With Us

Our response to God's work (our service to him) corresponds to his service to us and gives us this three-fold sequence:

We Confess Our Sins
We Respond in Prayer and Offering
We Feed on Jesus.

If we put this all together and include the call to worship at the beginning and the blessing or commissioning of God at the end, then we have the following five-fold order of sacrificial or covenant renewal worship:

**God Calls Us**
    We Gather Together and Praise Him
**God Cleanses Us**
    We Confess Our Sins

**God Consecrates Us**
    We Respond in Prayer and Offering

**God Communes with Us**
    We Eat and Drink with the Lord and
    One Another

**God Commissions (Blesses) Us**
    We March Out to Serve God

The liturgy moves from tension to rest, from mourning to joy. God calls us together, cleans us up, tells us how to live, fuels us for service in his kingdom, and sends us forth. We strip off our soiled garments, are washed clean by the blood of Christ, are given white robes of holiness and authority, wedding garments of glory for the meal, and finally, because of our worship, we are fitted out with armor to carry out our mission in the world. This is what happens to us in sacrificial, covenant renewal worship.

## The Lord's Supper as Covenant Memorial

When understood against the backdrop of all the Old Testament memorials, the Lord's Supper as a "memorial" is shown to be first a dramatized ritual prayer reminding God of his covenant. The Lord's Supper is the New Covenant Memorial. It is the fulfillment of all the older ways which the Lord instituted as the means whereby his people would call upon his Name and dramatically ask him to *remember his covenant*. All the Old Covenant memorials are fulfilled and completed (compacted) in the one simple covenantal memorial meal of the New Covenant. Jesus says, "do this as my memorial" (Luke 22:19; 1 Cor. 11:24). This means that there are two major moments or actions in this Sacrament.

First, there is our memorializing of the death of Jesus. This is our action toward God, our prayer to God to remember Jesus and keep his covenant. We "show forth" the death of Jesus to the Father asking him to keep his gracious promises to us in Christ. In the case of the Lord's Supper this memorializing is an act of the congregation, a pleading of the promises of God. Here is the memorial of your Son's atoning sacrifice for us: O Lord, remember and be gracious towards us! This comes to focus in the prayer of thanksgiving (Greek: *eucharist*) and memorial. This prayer ought to include a summary of the life and work of Jesus Christ. This prayer and the *doing* of the Lord's Supper then "show forth the death of Jesus" (1 Cor. 11:26) to the Father. It is a dramatic prayer, a pleading of the promises of the Father by memorializing his Son's birth, life, suffering, death, and resurrection for us. That is the first major moment in the movement of the ritual of the Lord's Supper. We memorialize Jesus to the Father.

Second, there is God's faithful response to our plea. He remembers his covenant promises and comes in blessing for his people and in judgment on his enemies. Memorializing Jesus to the Father causes him to act, to come, to visit his people. This fits with the pattern in 1 Corinthians 11:17-34. God's coming in blessing, however, is not highlighted in the Corinthian church. Rather, because of their rebellion God was indeed coming, but coming in judgment (v. 29-30).

The Sacrament of Communion is connected not merely to the work of Christ in the past, but the Spirit communicates to us the life-giving, glorified, flesh of the resurrected and enthroned Christ in this Sacrament. How he does so is a miracle and therefore a mystery, but we receive it by faith. We receive the Bread, and as a community are (re)formed into his Body, and when we drink from the Cup we are, through the

Blood of the covenant shed for our forgiveness, our-selves made into living sacrifices.

In summary, the Lord's Supper is both 1) a drama-tized, ritualized prayer, in which we call upon God to remember the sacrificial death of Jesus Christ to keep his covenant with us, and then 2) in response to our memorial prayer, God comes near to serve and nour-ish us with the life-giving nourishment available to us in Christ, reconstituting us as one body with his Son. The Lord's Supper marks the culmination of our being drawn into God's presence by way of sacrifice and there-by anticipates the Wedding Supper of the Lamb. At the Table the Church ritually anticipates the New Heavens and Earth, when she will participate in the Son's eucha-ristic offering of the entire creation to the Father.

We have a standing joke in our family when we get together for meals: We come together to eat and then we talk about eating at the table. I suspect that it is not much different for most families. We congre-gate around food, not just for nourishment but also for social reasons. Families unite around the table. Friendships are formed and cultivated at meals. Elab-orate social rituals develop to set apart common meals and to facilitate fellowship. We live to eat and eating structures our common life. This is how God has made us. This is why the covenant renewal service should not end with the sermon and offering. It should never end without Communion. God has called the church together to eat with him. There are other times when we can gather for teaching, testimonies, praise, or whatever. On the Lord's Day, God invites us to his house for a meal. Yes, he cleanses and consecrates us, but before God sends us out to serve him in the world, he sits us down for a common meal. He must strengthen and nourish us with bread and wine for service in his kingdom. We must experience the *shalom* of God at the Table. Therefore, the culmination of the covenant renewal service occurs when we relax and eat dinner with Jesus, receiving from him by faith his own life-giving flesh and blood.

# The Biblical Form
# of the Divine Service

*Let Israel now say that he is good: that his mercy endures forever.* —Psalm 118:2

I need to defend the *corporate* nature of our liturgy, specifically the use of coordinated, congregational prayer in our service. I am referring to the responses and prayers that the congregation recites together. My goal in this section is to discuss and defend the use of set or fixed congregational prayers—that is, printed prayers prayed in unison by the people. The question I want to answer in this section is a very common one: Why does the congregation often use printed, pre-composed prayers? Isn't spontaneous, free prayer more spiritual?

## The Heavenly Pattern

Jesus taught us to pray "Thy will be done on earth as it is in heaven" (Matt. 6:10). He thereby established heaven as the pattern for what is done on earth. (Actually, this pattern is symbolized in many places in the Old Testament, beginning in Genesis 1:1-2.) This is especially the case regarding the church's worship. Surely the way worship is conducted in heaven functions as a model for the church on earth. When the Apostle John was privileged to observe heavenly worship, as he records for us in the Revelation, he saw an *orderly, formal service* performed by angels, living beings, and the twenty-four elders (the precise identity of each of these beings is not our concern here). They repeated various rituals and ritual responses (Rev. 4:9-11). They alternated responses antiphonally (Rev. 5:11-14). They sang hymns in unison (Rev. 5:9). They fell down *together* (no doubt, a prearranged liturgical action), and they jointly recited prayers of praise and thanksgiving that must have been *pre-composed* and *memorized*. How else would they have all prayed (or sung) *simultaneously*? Here, then, we have a *biblical* model for corporate Lord's Day prayer in our worship services.

## An Unwarranted Assumption

Consider the way the question about pre-composed prayers is often asked. The question is often put in these terms: why does the congregation *read* these prayers? But are we *merely* reading them? No. The congregation does *not* just read these prayers, they *pray* them. One could just as well question the manner of praying at another church where the pastor does all the praying from the pulpit: why does that congregation merely *listen* to the pastor pray throughout the service? That would not be fair. The very way in which the question is put prejudices the case from the outset. Presumably, a congregation can pray *with* the pastor while he prays. The same ought to be true when the congregation *recites* prayers. Certainly, the congregation is able to do more than *merely* recite these prayers. They can make the written prayer their own. They can pray sincerely. In fact, I believe, practically speaking, that it is easier to pray sincerely when one takes up a written prayer on one's lips, than when one merely listens to another person pray.

## Is Bodily Posture Important?

But all this talk about responses and printed prayers seems more Anglican, Lutheran, and Catholic than Presbyterian. Yes, Catholics, Lutherans, and Anglicans practice similar forms in their worship services. So what? Does that make it wrong? Roman Catholics and Episcopalians kneel for prayer; does that make kneeling dangerous or wrong? I always chuckle a little inside whenever a pastor calls a congregation to worship on Sunday morning using Psalm 95: 6—"Oh, come let us worship and bow down; let us kneel before the Lord our maker"—and then the congregation stands or remain seated. Why not kneel in worship like the Bible directs? I suspect that one of the reasons is that we are afraid that we might look like Roman Catholics or Episcopalians. As far as I'm concerned, that's a pitiful reason for not obeying the Bible.

Of course, kneelers in the pews would help. During the confession of sin the congregation *ought* to be on their knees, but, alas, our tradition has largely ignored the need for kneelers because it has failed to guard and pass on the biblical teaching and the traditional Christian practice regarding the importance of bodily posture throughout the entire worship service. I have heard people say that God is not interested in the posture of our bodies, but only the attitude of our hearts. Well, that's not exactly what the Bible says. There are too many references in the Bible to outward bodily postures in worship to dismiss kneeling as mere formalism.

What most people fail to recognize is that one's bodily posture will both express and help establish the posture of one's heart. When we are humbled, we hang our heads. When we are joyful, our arms and head fly up and we begin to move. More often than not, the reason most American Protestants don't kneel in worship is not because they are too humble, but too proud. It is all too convenient for us to keep to ourselves and not reveal our true selves in such bodily postures. This is pride. After citing numerous biblical references, Robert S. Rayburn notes,

> . . . the position of the body is itself an act of worship. When you kneel or stand because you are in the presence of the Almighty and are to speak to him, you are honoring him with your entire self, with your soul and body together expressing reverence. In Holy Scripture, whenever men or women came face to face with God, they always immediately and instinctively assumed postures which were appropriate for a creature and a sinner before the living God. . . If we are really worshiping God as his children, then we are to worship him not with half ourselves but with our whole selves and our bodies ought to be as involved as our souls. . . This was the feeling of the church in the days of the Reformation.

A failure to take proper positions of body in the church was regarded as an act of irreverence."[1]

Rayburn also quotes from the older *Book of Discipline of the French Reformed Church* (1559):

That great irreverence which is found in divers persons, who at public and private prayers do neither uncover their heads nor bow their knees shall be reformed; which is a matter repugnant unto piety, and giveth suspicion of pride, and scandalizes them that fear God. Wherefore all pastors shall be advised, as also elders and heads of families, carefully to oversee, that in time of prayer all persons, without exception do evidence by these exterior signs the inward humility of their hearts and homage which they yield to God; unless anyone be hindered from doing so by sickness or otherwise."[2]

---

1. "Worship and the Whole Man," *The Second Annual Conference on Worship: The Theology and Music of Reformed Worship, February 23-25, 1996* (Nashville, TN: Covenant Presbyterian Church, 1996), 42, 43.

2. Chapt. 10, Art. 1.

Many modern Reformed folk are surprised that congregations in Reformation churches knelt for prayer. It would have been hard for Reformers to conceive of any other posture for prayer (besides standing, of course). Nobody sat for prayer. Calvin and Luther would have been baffled at our arrogant refusal to practice what the Bible instructs merely to avoid being identified with another branch of the church, however wrong that church may be about other doctrinal matters.

**The Reformation and the Priesthood of All Believers**
One of the central intentions of the sixteenth century Reformers remains virtually unknown in many of our churches today. The reformers to a man, especially Luther and Calvin, sought to correct the late medieval distortions of worship by restoring *congregational participation*. The late medieval mass was hardly a *congregational* worship service at all. The service was said in Latin, which very few laymen understood. There was virtually no congregational participation in the service beyond *watching* the visual "performance" by the priest at the altar. The bread, (supposedly) transformed into Christ's real body, held up for the people to adore, was the climax of the mass. The people almost never partook of the Communion elements; only the priest ate

and drank. There were no congregational prayers or singing or recitation of the creeds. The congregation merely watched and listened. They were largely passive. As *individuals* they may have performed private devotions completely independent of what the priest was doing up front, but as a *community* they did not participate in the liturgy.

To the Reformers this was a gross distortion of biblical and early church (second-third century) worship practices. One of their greatest achievements was to restore intelligent, unified participation by the body of Christ in worship. They transformed the people from uncomprehending observers of the worship of the sacrificing priests into an active royal priesthood. Calvin, echoing the early church fathers, insisted that "each Christian bears the exalted title of sacrificer," and therefore has a rightful place in the *offering* of praise and prayer in the liturgy. It is not the priest alone who has access into the heavenly sanctuary, but rather every member of the body of Christ has heavenly access into God's throne room on the Lord's Day. In the New Covenant there are no degrees of nearness (as there were in the Old Covenant), but every worshiper is a "saint," that is, one who has *sanctuary* access.

This, of course, is the great Reformation principle of the *priesthood of all believers*. The principal manifestation and evidence of the reality of this fundamental truth takes place during corporate worship as the whole congregation *participates* in offering to God prayer and praise. The congregation prays, praises, and communes with God. The pastor does not worship *for* them as a proxy; the people worship as the pastor *leads* them. What this means is that the priesthood of all believers demands a corporate liturgy!

Thus, the Reformers restored many of the pre-medieval practices of the post-Apostolic church. They intentionally sought to recover what has been called "Old Catholic" forms of worship while bypassing the distortions of medieval *Roman* Catholic liturgical rites. The Reformers restored frequent Communion. They all sought to reintroduce *weekly* Communion at every Lord's Day worship service. They all effectively revived preaching and teaching so that the people could be instructed by God's Word every week. They all brought the recitation of the creeds by the congregation back into the worship service. They all rediscovered the inspired Psalms as the prayer and hymn book for the entire Church (not just the priests, monks, and nuns).

Moreover, congregational singing was resurrected and became one of the hallmarks of Reformation worship. Calvin discusses music and singing under the heading of *prayer*. The people were taught to sing the

Psalms in corporate worship, since the Psalter is the *prayer book* of the Bible. All the Reformers wrote model liturgies and prayers for use in the churches. This revival of congregational prayer was based squarely on the priesthood of all believers, which demanded that the people *participate* in the prayers and not just *listen* to them. In fact, the liturgies of the Reformers, Calvin included, were much more fixed than we modern Americans would feel comfortable with. The point I am trying to make here, though, is that congregational praying of pre-composed prayers, either spoken or sung, has a long and venerable history in Reformation churches and ought not to be jettisoned merely because they are not familiar forms to modern American Presbyterians.

### Exposing an Absurd Objection

Back to the main issue. What about pre-composed prayers recited by the congregation? I often hear a complaint that runs like this: "How can I pray what someone else wrote? These words are being *forced* on me. They are not coming from my heart and so I should not be made to pray them. I am against all forms of liturgies that are imposed on the congregation. They put the Spirit in a straitjacket." This kind of objection is often sincere and well meaning, but to be frank, it is easily reduced to absurdity.

If the only prayer that a participant in the congregation can pray during a worship service is one which comes spontaneously from the individual worshiper's heart, then *congregational* worship as such is ruled out. *People must do things together in congregational worship.* The people of God gather *together* as a *community* to offer unified prayer and praise to the Father through the Son in the power of the Holy Spirit. If all prearranged liturgies and prayers *per se* are impositions on the individual worshiper's freedom, then the only thing left is for everyone to gather and worship the Lord spontaneously as individuals. But even then you run into trouble. If worship must be free in the sense that no external forms are allowed whatsoever, then no one, not the pastor, nor anyone in the congregation could ever be allowed to impose *any* form on *anyone* in the congregation, except possibly if a unanimous vote was taken each time a suggestion was made. To press a little more, *someone* would have to determine the *time* to begin the service, and this would be an artificially imposed regulation that would shackle the Spirit's freedom. Some people may not be ready to worship at 9:00 a.m.! Why restrict their freedom in the Spirit?

We must be clear on this point. If one objects to pre-composed prayers because one believes they unnecessarily bind the conscience of the believer to a particular form, then logically one must also reject all hymns, all prayers spoken by the pastor, and, indeed, any *order* of service whatsoever. If pre-composed spoken prayers are a hindrance to the spontaneity of the Spirit, then so are pre-composed *sung* prayers—hymns! After all, hymns are prayers—pre-composed prayers. Singing is just a heightened form of speech—glorified and beautified speech. Not many people ever really think clearly about this. There is no fundamental difference between a congregational prayer *recited* in unison by the people and one that is *sung* in unison by the people. Make no mistake about it, hymns are pre-composed prayers of praise or petition written (usually) by someone outside of the congregation and "imposed" on the people by whoever prepares the bulletin. These hymns (to continue our *reductio ad absurdum* argument) then become an imposed, alien form which stifles the freedom of the Spirit and hinders all heartfelt spontaneity. Logically, as I indicated above, one would also be forced to reject all prayers by the pastor as well, since the pastor's prayers are nothing but an external form of prayer imposed on the congregation. I think you get the point now. Formal prayer is not necessarily the same as formal*ism*.

## Corporate Prayer in the Bible

Pre-composed prayers are Biblical. This practice is not merely some leftover from Roman Catholicism. Our use of set prayers is very self-conscious. The historical church got the idea from the Bible, particularly the Psalms and the book of Revelation, but not exclusively so. The Old Testament is filled with examples of how the saints used set forms of prayer to confess and praise God (Ezra 3:10; Neh. 12:24; Ps. 136). David appointed Levites to compose prayers and songs to be used in the corporate worship of Israel (I Chron. 6:31-48; 15:16-24; 16:4-6; 25:1-5). These prayers and songs were then preserved for corporate use by the Israelites during their weekly and annual worship services (Lev. 23). Moved by the Holy Spirit, David himself composed prayers for corporate and individual use (I Chron. 16:7). Do not miss my point. The *Holy Spirit* moved David to compose and preserve for posterity a corporate prayer book for the saints. David in his Spirit-guided wisdom appointed Spirit-filled men to compose a song book/prayer book for the people to aid them in their public as well as private worship.

The Psalm titles, contents, and structure all witness to the fact that they were used primarily by the community of faith in corporate worship. Just scanning through the Psalms one finds that many of them begin with words like "A Psalm for the Sabbath Day" (Ps. 92) or "To the Chief Musician: A Psalm of the sons of Korah" (Ps. 47). The *content* of many of the Psalms also witnesses to their intended use in public worship: hymns of praise (Ps. 95, 145-150), community confessions (Ps. 78, 105, 106, 135), and Psalms to be sung as the people ascend to Jerusalem for worship (Ps. 120-134).

Notice the many references to *specific postures* of worship within the Psalms (Ps. 5:7, Ps. 63:2-3, Ps. 95: 6, "O come let us worship and bow down, let us kneel before the Lord our Maker"). Even the *very structure* of the poetry supports its appropriateness for responsive and antiphonal recitation and singing in worship. They were written for congregational recitation and singing. Their structure testifies to the fact that the Spirit composed them to be recited and sung responsively or antiphonally in congregational worship (Neh. 12:24). Psalm 136 is an obvious example, cast as it is in the form of a litany:

Give thanks to the LORD, for he is good,
    for his steadfast love endures forever.
Give thanks to the God of gods,
    for his steadfast love endures forever.
Give thanks to the Lord of lords,
    for his steadfast love endures forever;

So, when we use the Psalms in worship, whether we are reciting them in unison, reciting them antiphonally or responsively, or whether we are praying them by singing them, by so doing we are following God's appointed forms of worship. Furthermore, when we include in the service Psalm-like prayers to be said by the congregation in unison, we are seeking to follow biblical guidelines that enable the congregation to *participate together* as a community in the *activity* of worshiping the Lord.

These kinds of prayers also help to guide and *train* the congregation in the art of biblical praying. We do not "naturally" know *how* to pray. The fact that one is a Christian does not guarantee that he will know how to pray. There is a silly myth that goes pretty much unchallenged in American Evangelicalism—that worship comes "naturally." As a friend once nicely put it: "Christians have to be taught everything from how to study the Bible to how to love their wives, husbands, and children. But when it comes to worship, evangelicals are nervous about someone teaching them prayers, chants, and even a 'set form of worship.' Worship is supposedly the one thing that every living, breathing Christian automatically does the right way." This is a myth, a dangerous myth. When I look at the Bible I see all kinds of instruction and forms given to help us learn *how* to approach the King of Kings properly. Coming into God's presence is different from anything else we do, and it is one of the most difficult activities we do.

Consider again what we discover when we look into *heaven* and see how worship is conducted there. Lo and behold, we hear prayers spoken or sung *in unison* by great throngs of people and angels (Rev. 4 & 5). Notice that heavenly worship is conducted with set prayers and responses. How else would they all know what to say and when to say it? In heaven the saints triumphant pray responsively and antiphonally in concert with the angels. Remember that Jesus taught us to pray "Thy will be done on earth as it is in heaven." Earthly congregational praying ought to be modeled on heavenly congregational praying!

## The Usefulness of Congregational Prayers

Finally, summing up our argument so far, pre-composed, congregational prayers are a valuable aid to worship. How so? First, we don't know how to pray, and pre-composed prayers can help train our minds to pray biblically. Good prayers guide us and assist us in composing our own prayers, both with respect to content and structure. Almost all the phrases from all the prayers that we use in our worship come right out of the Bible. Thus, ultimately, we are praying God's Word. There *are* biblical ways to pray, and these pre-composed prayers, used consistently, will help you *learn* how to pray. Surely that's the reason why so many prayers are recorded for us in the Bible. These prayers offer the worshiper guidance and direction, oftentimes by utilizing the language and structure (order of prayer) lifted right from the Bible itself.

Second, prayers sung or said in unison manifest the *unity of the church* in prayer. We all pray *together* as the corporate body of Christ, not just as a bunch of individuals. Corporate worship is not designed merely as an aid to each individual's devotions. We don't come into church to worship merely as individuals with our own private tubes to God. We come together as the body of Christ, and as the body of Christ we confess our sins, pray, and praise God together. The Spirit re-creates us into a community.

Third, printed prayers ensure congregational participation in the prayers. Remember worship ought not to be something you come to watch or hear; rather you come to perform worship yourself. Think about this: it is very difficult to get distracted when you are saying a prayer out loud. It is hard to do anything else but pray the prayer. A set prayer ensures your participation and guards against your mind wandering. I submit to you that it is much more difficult for your mind to wander when your attention is focused on *reading* and *saying* a prayer that you are holding in front of you than it is when you have your eyes closed and are merely listening to the pastor pray. Let's face it—most people find it very difficult to concentrate on praying when someone else is saying a long prayer.

Fourth, no church can avoid prayer rituals altogether. You either have *good* prayer rituals or you have *bad* ones, helpful or dangerous ones, but it is impossible to be free from all *forms* in a church's corporate prayer life. Congregations that never use prayer books or set prayers, nevertheless, *do* develop, sometimes unknowingly (which is unfortunate), certain habits with respect to praying. You know very well what happens when there is no guidance or direction to the prayers. Prayers become tedious: "I *just* want to thank you, Lord. . . and I *just* want to ask. . . and I *just* want. . ." Or they become trivial and down right silly: "O Lord, help us to *be all that we can be*" (the *Army* Prayer) or "Lord, help us to *reach out and touch somebody* this week" (the *AT&T* prayer).

Now, of course, we are not obliged to use all kinds of pretentious words and grandiose phrases in order for our prayers to be acceptable to God. I'm not trying to put down anyone's prayer merely because it is not as well structured and manicured as someone else's. God is pleased with the meager and unsophisticated prayers of his people, just as he is pleased with a young child's. But—and here's the important point—if the child never grows up and learns how to pray biblically, if the *content* of his prayers remain the same, then it is not so cute anymore. God may be *pleased* with a childlike prayer, but he is not *satisfied* with it either. He expects us to grow up and learn how to pray like adults, to conform our prayers more and more to the models he has given us in the Scriptures.

Some churches never get beyond praying for sick people and saying grace at the table. That's fine as far as it goes, but have you ever noticed that the Bible does not contain a whole lot of prayers for sick people and pretty much assumes that we know how to give thanks for our food? Again, I'm not talking here about a fancy, flowing style. My concern centers on the *content* of the prayers: confession of sin; thanking God for creation and providence; thanking God for the person and work of Christ; praying for strength in the midst of temptation; praying that His kingdom would be protected from all its enemies and extended throughout the world. These are petitions that do not come "naturally" to us. We need to be trained. Printed, set prayers help to discipline and educate us. They help us to grow up and pray like mature Christians.

### Only the Lover Sings
Somewhere Augustine sloganizes the importance of singing: *Cantare amantis est* (Latin: "only the lover sings"). Lovers don't merely talk, they sing. We sing to those we love. We sing about that which we love. Love beautifies. Just as poetry is glorified written communication, singing is appropriate whenever plain talk is not enough. It would be wonderful if our churches could sing most, if not all of the liturgy. After all, why *say* it when you can *sing* it? James Hastings Nichols describes the typical Reformation service in the 16th century:

> In classical Reformed worship the 'liturgy' in the strict sense, the people's part, was all sung. It is not the spoken prayers, taken by the minister, but the sung liturgy of the people which must be studied in the first instance to comprehend the meaning of early Reformed worship.

That may come as a surprise to modern Protestants. We typically say everything and then only sing the hymns. Colossians 2:15-17, however, commends us to let the word of Christ dwell in us "richly" by singing "psalms, hymns, and Spiritual songs." The Word dwells in our midst richly or gloriously when it is sung. Singing glorifies and beautifies speech. When you love someone, you use heightened, glorified poetic speech and you sing those words to your lover!

The Lord's Day service is the context where we express our gratitude and love for God. Here we are called to glorify God with our speech. Adoration is a state of the soul that only singing can appropriately express. Follow the progression:

1. Poetry is glorified words.

2. Glorified words are glorified still more when they are sung.

3. The union of many voices makes singing even more glorious.

4. Still again, complex harmonies glorify congregational singing.

5. Finally, the sung word is made yet more glorious when accompanied by instrumental music.

Such a rich conception of congregational participation is true to the best in Reformation theology and practice. For example, a steady stream of men were trained in Calvin's Geneva and sent out as missionaries into all of Europe to establish the Gospel. The Reformation was not simply an intellectual, doctrinal movement—a mere attempt to propagate ideas or doctrines. The Reformation, whether led by Luther or Calvin, was a full-fledged liturgical reformation.

You didn't just come to Calvin's Geneva in the 1500s to learn doctrine; you came to learn how to worship God. You came to be formed into a worshiping community. You were trained to sing. To sing your faith! To sing the Apostles' and Nicene Creeds. To sing the Word of God. To sing your prayers. To sing the Lord's Prayer. Especially, to sing the inspired hymnbook of the Church, the Psalter. You were trained in a new manner of living fitting for the Gospel. You were trained to be incorporated into a Christian army of Psalm-singing worshipers. This is what it means to be a Reformation Christian. You are a singing Christian, a participant in a congregation of singing, justified believers. The bottom line: given the example of our fathers in the early church and Reformed tradition, we should learn to sing more of the Lord's Service.

# Brief Answers to Frequently Asked Questions

*A question is a trap, and an answer your foot in it.*
— John Steinbeck, *Travels with Charley*

### Why do we say or sing the Nicene Creed?

The English word "creed" comes from the Latin *credo*, which means "I believe" or "I trust" or even "I place my faith in." We confess the ancient Nicene Creed as our pledge of loyalty to the Triune God. The Creed is not a list of "doctrines" but a recitation of the gracious acts of God for us, as well as what we hope for from him in the future.

### Why do we sing Psalms every week?

We sing Psalms because these are the sung prayers that God has given to Israel and the church. The Psalms give us words to express the full range of human emotions in prayer to God. When we have the words of the Psalms in our minds and hearts, we have divinely authorized content and forms for prayer.

### Why do we chant some of the Psalms?

When we "chant" the Psalms we are sticking very close to the inspired text and not changing the words to make lines rhyme and/or to fit predetermined metrical music. The poetic flow of the words in Hebrew is part of the inspired text and communicates more than simply ideas.

### Why do we kneel for confession?

Because we worship not just with our mind but with our body. When the Scriptures record encounters with God or the risen Christ people go down on their faces or knees. Not only does lowering the body express humility and repentance, but it also helps us get into a humble frame of mind to confess our sins.

### Why does the service move so quickly?
### And why are hymns sung at such a rapid tempo?

Worship ought to be lively and energetic because we are in the presence of the living God. How the service is *performed* is important. When pastors lead the service too quietly and slowly, the dance-like character of the interaction between the Lord and his people is lost.

Too many "traditional services" are performed poorly and that is often the reason why folks judge liturgical services as "boring." Some hymns, of course, are better sung a bit more slowly, especially those that involve either confession or contemplation. But most hymns are meant to be sung energetically and with passionate praise.

### Why do we sing so many older hymns?

The Holy Spirit has confirmed the use of many of these hymns because the Church has sung them for centuries. Traditional hymns are rich with biblical theology that engages our minds as well as our hearts. Letting the wisdom of older saints guide us in the modern Church expresses our humility and receptivity to the wisdom of Christian tradition as the Spirit has led the Church.

### Why does everyone talk to each other while the wine is being distributed at Communion?

When we eat dinner at home around the family table, we talk to each other. Unless you are eating alone, silence at the table means something is wrong. When we eat the Lord's Supper we are not merely communing as individuals, as if we all have our own private tubes into heaven. We are eating as a community, as a body, so it is very appropriate to acknowledge the presence of those around you and pass "the peace of Christ" to them.

### Why does the pastor wear a white robe?

The pastor wears the uniform of his calling in the service to remind everyone that everything he says and does in leading the service is performed in his official capacity as a minister of Jesus Christ. He's not a businessman, so he doesn't wear a suit and tie. He's not a comedian or entertainer, so he doesn't wear casual clothes or jeans and a T-shirt. He's not a judge or an academic, so he doesn't wear a black robe. He's a pastor to the congregation. As has been the traditional practice in most churches for centuries, he wears a white robe with a stole colored according to the appropriate season in the church year. Just as uniforms identify doctors, nurses, judges, policemen, repairmen, even UPS drivers, so also a uniform is appropriate to help identify Christian pastors.

### Why do we follow the church year?

The Apostle Paul tells us that "everything God has created is good and nothing is to be rejected if it is received with thanksgiving, for it is sanctified by the word of God and prayer" (1 Tim. 4:4-5). The church sanctifies time, specifically the yearly cycles of our life, with the word of God and prayer. We coordinate God's created, recurring seasonal cycles with Scripture readings and prayer to remember the life of Jesus Christ. It has only been since the French Revolution (AD 1789) that the calendar has been secularized in so many countries. No longer is it keyed primarily to the great redemptive historical events of Christ's life, death and resurrection. The calendar has been de-Christianized and politicized. But we think there's a better way to mark time that transcends nationalism and the veneration of political heroes.

# A Short Glossary of Terms Often Used in the Service

*Every word is a name. . .*
—Augustine, *On the Teacher*

### Covenant

The Scriptures designate God's personal relationship with us as a covenant. A covenant is a formal personal bond, which has an objective shape and configuration, with promises, obligations, rituals, symbols, etc. Marriage is an example of a covenantal relationship. Sunday worship is called a "covenant renewal" because God graciously renews his relationship with us by drawing us near by means of his covenantal Word and sacramental rituals.

## Salutation

Another Latin term that refers to the "greeting" at the beginning of the service. The pastor says, "The Lord be with you," and the people respond, "and also with you" or "and with your spirit." This establishes a bond between the people and the minister at the start of the service.

## Sanctus

The Latin term for "holy." This is the seraphic song that Isaiah hears in chapter 6, but also sung by the angels in heaven in Revelation 5. The song combines the angelic chorus with the petitions of the people at the arrival of Jesus in Jerusalem: "Hosanna in the Highest." Hosanna is the Hebrew petition to "deliver" or "save."

## Purification

This is the name of the first "sacrifice" made in the sequence of animal sacrifices given to Israel as the way of drawing near to the Lord. This particular sacrifice highlights the death of the animal (symbolizing the worshiper) and the disposition of blood on the altar (a public display that the death has happened) in order to begin the process of the ascension into the Lord's presence.

## Yahweh

Yahweh is the revealed name of God in the Hebrew Scriptures. The English word "God" is a generic term for divinity, a translation of the Hebrew *El* or *Elohim*. The true God revealed his personal name "Yahweh" to his covenant people so they could call on him by name. The Jews later decided that it was too dangerous to say that name and instead said *Adonai* (Lord) whenever the name Yahweh occurred in the Scriptures. Unfortunately, English translations perpetuate that superstition by translating Yahweh as "Lord." But God's *name* is not Lord. Lord is another word for Master. That's simply one of his *titles*. Our Lord and God is Yahweh. And Yahweh came to us in the flesh. The name "Jesus" is the English way of saying "Joshua," and that Hebrew name means "Yahweh saves" (*Yah-shua*).

## Consecration

From the Latin that means "set apart" or "make holy." After we are purified, we are consecrated by the Word of God. During this part of the service we hear the Scriptures read and explained and are thereby exposed to the consecrating power of the Word of God. This corresponds to the priestly preparation of the animal for its ascent to the altar.

### *Sursum Corda*

From the Latin "lifted hearts." It is often put just before Communion; but may also be placed near the beginning, after we are forgiven, to highlight that God has drawn us up and near to him at the start of the service. When we say, "We lift up our hearts before the Lord" we are confessing by faith that we have been admitted into the Lord's heavenly court "with angels and archangels and all the company of heaven."

### Psalm Chants

The word "chant" has a medieval ring to it and so may be misunderstood by modern Christians. But we often chant Psalms in order to stay very close to the actual inspired words of the Psalms, which is the sung prayerbook that God has given to his people. In other words, chanting Psalms enables us to sing God's Word without altering it to fit a predetermined metrical tune.

### Nicene Creed

A creed is a spoken or sung confession of faith (*credo* is Latin for "I believe" or "I trust"). The Nicene Creed was written in 381 AD and has been used in the liturgy of the church ever since. We are proclaiming our trust in the God who has acted for us, from creation to the resurrection. The creed is not a list of doctrines, but a recitation of the mighty acts of God in history.

### Te Deum

The first words of the ancient fourth-century hymn we may sing in place of a creed. *Te Deum laudamus* is Latin for "O God, we praise Thee."

### Kyrie

From the Greek for "O Lord." The Kyrie is an ancient sung prayer for mercy. This is not a prayer for forgiveness (which has already been extended), but for God to graciously help us praise him and that our service to him would benefit not only ourselves but the world.

### Lectionary

The way the church orders her Scripture readings is called "the lectionary" (from the Latin *lectio*, a "reading"). We commonly use the Revised Common Lectionary (RCL) during the seasons of Advent, Christmas, Epiphany, Lent, and Easter. But oftentimes the Scripture readings are tied to the sermon text.

### Gloria Patri

Latin for "Glory to the Father." We often sing the *Gloria* after the Scripture readings and our confession of faith as a way of ascribing all glory to the Triune God for the gift of his wise counsel to us from his Word.

### Doxology

From the Greek: "words of glory." We praise God from whom all blessings flow immediately before we offer him our tribute, thereby confessing that everything we have comes from his gracious hand.

### Tribute Offering

In the sacrificial sequence this is the time when a meal offering is placed on top of the prepared animal sacrifice before it ascends to the fiery presence of God on the altar. Once our sins are forgiven and we have heard the Scriptures read and explained, we then offer ourselves to the Lord as we give our tithes and offerings. The Lord accepts the work of our hands and uses our gifts to advance his kingdom.

### Tithe

The word "tithe" comes from an Old English word that means "a tenth." The Lord asks us to acknowledge his benevolence toward us by designating ten percent of our increase as his tribute.

## Sacrifice of Peace

This is how the last offering in the sequence of animal offerings is designated. The final act of God is to give "peace" to his people as they eat and drink with him, enjoying meat cooked on the altar. After we are cleansed, consecrated, and offer our tribute, we sit down and enjoy the peace offered to us at the Table of the Lord.

## Eucharist

From the Greek for "Thanksgiving." The Apostle Paul uses this word to describe the Lord's Supper as a thanksgiving meal in 1 Corinthians 10.

## Memorial

The Lord's Supper is a memorial meal, but not primarily because it's given for us to remember. Rather, when we do and say what our Lord has given us to do and say we remind God of his covenant promises to come to our aid. We memorialize God, asking him to remember the suffering, death and resurrection of Jesus and be faithful to his promise to be with us. His gracious response to our memorial is to be present with us around the Table as we eat and drink the bread and wine.

## *Nunc Dimittis*

The Latin translation for the first words of Simeon's song in Luke 2. We sing this song at the end of the service because we have experienced the glory of the Lord and depart from the service in peace.

## Benediction

From the Latin for "good word." At the end of the service the minister places the blessing of God on the people and sends them out for service under God's protection. The traditional benediction used in the Church is the Aaronic blessing found in Numbers 6:24-26: "The Lord bless you and guard you. . ."

# A Closing Personal Note

*from Pastor Jeff Meyers*

I grew up in a very traditional liturgical church. The service was highly structured and mostly sung by the pastor and people. It followed the traditional order I have described in this booklet, even if some of the content was slightly different. I was baptized in that church and participated weekly in the service according to my capacity as a baby, toddler, young boy, and a teenager. Truth be told, as a young boy I was not always fully engaged in the service. I could get distracted easily. I remember daydreaming about having my BB gun in the sanctuary and knocking out panes of stained-glass windows one by one. Even so, I learned my part because of the *repetition* present in the worship. Everybody participated, children included. Every week I heard the Bible read, explained, prayed, and sung. I sang the classic hymns and learned to recite from memory the portions of Scripture embedded in the liturgy, as well as the Nicene Creed.

But in my first years of college no one who knew me would have said that all the "rote" worship really made much difference in my life. I was not attending church. I was walking away from the Christian life. I didn't attend worship services. But that changed. More accurately, the Lord changed me. He mercifully reeled me in and pulled me back from the precipice. This could be a long story, but all I want to do here is note how all the liturgy, Bible, creed and catechism recitation, psalm singing, and hymnody that was drilled into me in my formative years in the church—all of it came back to me when I walked into a Christian worship service again. Liturgical worship is a gift that will keep on giving. I have ministered to elderly Christians who could not remember much but would join in with prayers that they learned in church, hymns they regularly sang, and even portions of the liturgy that were repeated every week. Liturgical worship calibrates our minds and hearts to worship, live, and die as faithful Christians.

# Books for Further Study

*When you come, bring . . .*
*the books, and above all the parchments.*
—2 Timothy 4:13


Meyers, Jeffrey J. *The Lord's Service: The Grace of Covenant Renewal Worship*. Moscow, ID: Canon Press, 2003.

Lusk, Rich. *Measures of the Mission: A Survey of the Bible, Church, and Family*. Monroe, LA: Athanasius Press, 2023. Read this to understand the place of covenant renewal worship in the broader mission of the church.

Leithart, Peter J. *Theopolitan Liturgy*. Monroe, LA: Athanasius Press, 2021. Leithart provides us with an easy-to-read overview of the biblical theological foundation for covenant renewal worship.

Paquier, Richard. *Dynamics of Worship: Foundations and Uses of Liturgy*. Translated by Donald Macleod. Philadelphia: Fortress Press, 1967. The French Reformed theologian Paquier taps into the older, "continental" Calvinistic tradition that takes seriously questions of ritual, dress, bodily posture, sacraments, architecture, and the Church year—matters that are seldom addressed adequately in contemporary works on Reformed worship.

Jordan, James B. *The Liturgy Trap: The Bible Verses Mere Tradition in Worship*. Third Edition. Monroe, LA: Athanasius Press, 2008.

Gallant, Tim. *Baptism & Lord's Supper: A Biblical Primer on Covenant Initiation and Renewal*. Nashville, TN: Pactum Books, 2023. One of the best short introductions to the sacraments.

www.ingramcontent.com/pod-product-compliance
Lightning Source LLC
Chambersburg PA
CBHW071104120626
46546CB00003B/1274